In Memory of Douglas Paul Barrett.
"I'm in danger, I see, of being included among the whimsical fellows."
~Secoma, 1956

This is the New Age. We are all friends here.
~Anonymous

Imagine a customer service call center that is as big as the United States but only employs the best of the best. It is a call center that has people of all kinds, of many places but has them working together. They work together for the purpose of supporting the customers or providing technical advice. While interconnected, none of the agents are sitting next to another. In fact, most of them are miles away from each other but are working on the same team. Connected by chat, virtual meeting rooms, and conference calls, these teams of support representatives make up the fabric of what is a new age workforce. While this type of workforce has been around for many years, it is a larger segment of the working world than you may think. They are quite possibly your neighbors. These people are what this book refers to as the WAH Professionals. Each of these customer service representatives, tech support agents, and billing support specialists are all interconnected through the same network but each are miles away from the next.

This miracle is what modern technology as brought us. Long gone are the days of massive buildings filled with cubicles. It is a rare find to have a call center assembled with hundreds of people answering the telephones at the same time. Such buildings are even harder to find in the United States. With the world growing smaller, the work force is expanding and home offices are more often used for employment. As a customer of the businesses you deal with, you may have called a customer service number and heard only the representative on the other end of the phone. While you will find that some call centers are quiet like that, it is likely that you are speaking to an agent working from home. This may cause some concern about your personal information but, these representatives will ensure the security of your information and can provide the confidence that it will not be compromised in anyway. While most will not let on that they are WAH Professionals, or work from home agents, they likely are.

Most Americans want to speak to a customer support agent that not only speaks English well, but also sounds like they are from the United States and not another country. It is also easier to talk to the customer support representatives when it sounds like you are talking with just that person and are not listening to a sea of voices in the background. It is becoming more common for companies to have a portion of their work force outsourced to professionals that work from the comfort of their own home instead of sending the jobs overseas. The overhead is cheaper and the companies do not have to own the extra real estate to encompass a call center for their customer service needs. Further, it is more economical and less expensive to have a remote work force than it is to outsource an entire customer service department to another country. They say the world is getting smaller and, with WAH Professionals, it is embracing the technological revolution that is coming with it. The person on the phone, while on the other side of the country, appears to be right there, and focused on just you, the customer.

Working from home is definitely a lifestyle and not something to consider on a whim. It takes a certain kind of person and a special commitment to the lifestyle for it to work. If it is something you are willing to work for, it can be a very rewarding career choice and it has many perks that come with it. Lifestyle changes are never easy and can take time to become accustomed to. Remember that when you run into difficulties and keep an open mind. As with any career choice, there are obstacles that can make things seem impossible but that open mind will enable you to make the right decisions and respond accordingly.

Whether you have worked from home or are seriously considering a job working from home, this book is for you. While not all inclusive, it attempts to give you a general overview of what it is like to be a WAH Professional and what it takes to become one and be successful. It covers what it is like to be a work at home professional from initiating the job hunt to working your work at home job and living the lifestyle. This book even touches on the lives of real work from home agents and what motivates them. The common theme here is that this career is a lifestyle and is not for everyone. Hopefully, the discussion in this book will help you make the transition as you start your journey to becoming a WAH Professional. If working from home ends up being a good fit for you, it can be rewarding and even lead to career options that you would never have thought possible. Move over brick and mortar, WAH Professionals have their fuzzy puppy slippers on and are ready to work!

Background about the author

I have always wanted to work from home. Even as a kid, it fit right into the person that I was growing up to be. I marched to the beat of a different drummer and working from home was something that nobody else (I knew) was doing. I thought it sounded neat to tell people that "I work from home." I admit that it is very different than what I envisioned. However, it turned out to be rewarding just the same. As a child, I imagined what it would be like to work from the comfort of my kitchen table or living room. I often pretended to waitress with my parents in the living room or play office as I imagined running the house from the corner where my table sat. For hours I would work at my little table with its piles of important papers. It was fun "working" like that. I told my mother that I did not need a car when I grew up because it eliminated the whole ordeal of loading up the car, fighting traffic, and packing your lunch every day. I found that part of working to be the least desirable of "what I wanted to be when I grew up." Therefore, I always left that part out of my play. Most children tend to do that unless they actually see their parents go through that section of the routine of going to work every day.

At that young age, the only exposure I had about working from home was bringing your work home in a brief case or running by the post office or bank before or after the traditional workday. I was not aware that there were people that worked from home and actually got paid to do so. I did not know that the first telephone operators operated switchboards in their kitchens connecting callers from one home to another. Remember watching the old shows where someone would pick up the phone in the kitchen and immediately get an operator. They called the operator by first name and said "June! Connect me to a7472 over in the County! I need to talk to Miriam!" That was someone talking to an operator that operated a huge switchboard in her kitchen. Proof that working from home has been something more than babysitting for a long time.

    Little did I know that there was still real work from home jobs and that I was going to seek them out very soon. When I turned working age, I started that quest and have experienced many things from telecommutes to 100% at home atmospheres. I have put miles on my car to bring work home and take it back as well as work from my computer and on the phone. The results of those experiences and resulting searches have compelled me to write this book to help you when you take on your own journey to becoming a WAH professional.

Introduction

Most of my working life, I strived to work from the comfort of my own home. I believed it to be more rewarding work doing it from home as well as easier to make yourself get up and go to work every day. While I have enjoyed jobs that I have worked outside my home, the jobs that I have worked from my home office have proven to be the most rewarding career options. This is not something for everyone but that one special personality can greatly benefit from working out of their home.

From catering to research, folding t-shirts and inbound customer service, there are a variety of options to choose from. I have worked from home off and on since I was sixteen years old. My most recent stint working from home has been since 2011. I now find it difficult to imagine doing a traditional 9-5 job outside my home office. It would be a big adjustment to return to the traditional workforce as I have come accustomed to the benefits of working from my home office. I love being able to have access to my own kitchen and not worry about who is going to take my lunch. No more wondering if that thing growing in the fridge is going to invade my lunch bag or grow out of the break room fridge. I certainly enjoy the convenience of my own rest room facilities. However, these are only a couple of the things I perceive as benefits while being a Work At Home Professional.

There are as many benefits to working from home as there are challenges. Some challenges are the requirements that each job has. Other challenges can be things like: where to set up your work at home space or what changes in your home need to be made to accommodate the job requirements. Like any job, working from home takes a strong work ethic and dedication. You also want to seriously consider any accommodations that need to be made that will enable you to work from home.

Workers who leave the house every day to go to their job have challenges that are unique to their respective situation. There is traffic, transportation, what to do for lunch, and your work environment. The rest of us, who choose to work from home, have our own challenges as well. There are unique requirements specific to the jobs we work. There is also the technology requirement to ensure you can connect to the workplace servers and do the job from the comfort of your home. Some people may even have to change the set up of their home to accommodate a home office area that is separate from the rest of the house. Others will simply set up in a lesser used area or bedroom to do their work. The options available to you in your preferred work location are limitless within the confines of your home and can be personalized to reflect your style or job preferences. Conversely, those that have to leave the home to go to work have limited choice in their workspace because the company has it already set up for them.

If you are considering a work from home position, you have started in the right place. It is not simply the act of looking for a new job and that working from home is the only option available. It is a big undertaking and there is much to consider before reporting to the first day of work. Further, there are companies out there that are advertising jobs that are not legitimate and you want to be careful. This book is not going to try to sell you a list of companies that are hiring nor is it going to convince you to send a specific dollar amount to some P.O. Box for obtaining more useless information. Its purpose is to arm you with the knowledge to determine whether or not working from home is the right career path. If it is, then you can use the knowledge shared here to make it a rewarding career experience.

When considering any new career, there are questions that you need to ask yourself to understand if you are the right person for the job. You also need to ask if the job is the right fit for you. Not everyone is made to work from home. Just saying "I work from home" may sound great but it is not what everyone envisions it to be. While this book will not cover everything, it attempts to discuss most of the things you encounter in your desire to find a job and become a Work At Home Professional. Once discovering that working from home is the right for you, this book will discuss the onboarding[1] process as well as the daily work you may experience. Then this book also discusses a day in the life of work from home professionals.

While each person is different, there is camaraderie among those that work from home. Networking and friendships are truly different than what you experience in life away from the computer. This is for the dedicated group of people that are the inspiration for the title of this book: The WAH Professionals.

---

[1] On boarding-This refers to the process of filling out paperwork and becoming employed by a company after interviewing and accepting the job offer.

Job Types

The next few sections will briefly discuss job types that I have encountered over the years in my search for my perfect fit. This is not an exhaustive list but gives a broad spectrum of jobs one may encounter in their career search. Not all the jobs listed are true money makers nor may they be 100% at home work but they are things that are considered at home jobs and are other things that can be done by the WAH Professional in the course of their career. There are even a few sections that discuss temporary or contract work that gets the WAH Professional out of the house. Getting out of the house will be discussed later on as it is important to those that work from home to get a change of scenery once in a while. Remember, this is not all inclusive and there may be other opportunities out there that are not mentioned here. Just keep the advice of later chapters in mind when exploring what is available to you.

Hosiery

My very first experience at working from home was folding socks and pantyhose. This was ok for me. I was still in school and was not sure what I wanted to do with my life. Folding hosiery was my initial exposure to working from home and, while I loved it, I knew there had to be more than menial millwork such as folding pantyhose. It was more involved than I would have liked and involved a lot of manual labor that I was not happy with. Don't get me wrong, millwork and piecework are great for some people and many people love doing this type of work but it was not my thing. I would drive to the mill; pick up the contract, supplies, and hose. Then bring it home, unload it, and the work would begin. I could do this anywhere in the house and just set it up where the notion struck me. I didn't have to worry about distractions and I could watch television or talk on the phone while I worked. I could also have company over and not have to be secluded while I worked on the current project. While I needed lots of space when I brought home big jobs, I could clean up and put it in the corner when I was done for the day. I was still living with my parents, so I had to be respectful of their house and space. There was not a lot of conflict about where I worked so long as I cleaned up my mess when I was finished.

Lots of extra "unpaid" work went into this. Also, the pay was contract work.[2] This means it was basically piecework and not high pay. I paid my own gas, wear and tear on my car, and the only thing I received for compensation was around $0.10-$0.50 a dozen. When I finished the quota that I signed up for, I loaded everything back up in the car and took it all back to the mill and let the mill supervisor look at my work. If it was acceptable, I would sign my work sheet and come back in three days to pick up my check.

Another thing that made this a challenge was that there was a deadline of 72 hours. If you were late with your work, you did that work for free. Also, your work had

---

[2] Contract work is generally paid in cash or without a traditional pay check. Upon reaching a certain dollar amount, you may have to pay your own taxes on the monies earned. In 2013, $600 was the threshold for South Carolina where you start to pay taxes on self-employed earnings. Please check your state and federal guidelines for paying taxes on amounts earned that are considered "self-employed" earnings. Further, earnings are considered as self-employed earnings or contract work if the employer does not take out taxes. If the employer does not tax your pay, then you are responsible for paying taxes on monies earned.

to be beyond exceptional to be considered for the higher paying contracts. You could do standard work and still get the lower paying contracts. I imagine that is ok if you lived next door to the mill and travel was not an issue. Sometimes, socks would be set at $0.05 a dozen. Socks were easy work and did not take long but you had to do a lot of them to get any substantial amount of pay. Personally, I never chose anything less than fifteen cents per dozen and often tried to get the larger contracts with the higher pay. I was once offered a one-time contract for folding t-shirts for $2.00 a dozen. It was an emergency contract and had to be returned in 24 hours. It paid ok for that one time but I had been turning out good work for about 2 years before they offered me work like that.

     I think I would have stayed with it longer had I been offered more work with higher pay. However, it was not something that was going to pay the bills for the long term. Later, I would go back to that when I needed money outside of my regular full-time job. Any extraneous expenses were out of my pocket and it was something for extra spending money. There was not much of a paycheck after you consider the expense. They DID like my work, which meant I got priority choice of contracts. However, the novelty of folding hose and socks eventually wore out. I would do it again if I needed to. However, this type of work is only in certain locales. Sadly, it is not available in the area I live anymore.

Phone books

One opportunity that bears mentioning is one that you can do in one or two days. This opportunity happens every spring and it is a great way to earn a quick buck. It can also give you a change of pace. Anyone who has searched the classifieds of the local newspaper has seen the springtime ads for phone book delivery. While this is not quite a work from home job, it gets WAH professionals out of the house for a few hours one or two days and you get paid for tossing books. The routes for these are paid based on the number of books delivered and the size of the route. Phone book delivery is considered contract work and taxes are not taken out of the pay earned. Also, it is not a long-term job.

When I delivered phone books, they paid mileage and per book. You signed up for the routes you were interested in and delivered the books. After they did a random verification check, you could pick up your check the following week. As previously mentioned, delivering phone books is contract work and the routes run from about $35.00-$100.00. These routes or combination of routes can take anywhere from a couple of hours to a full day. Not difficult to accomplish. While delivering phone books is not for everyone, it is something you can do to get some money within about a week. For those that are truly WAH professionals, it is a nice change of pace. Even if it only comes around once or twice a year, it can be a sanity saver. As discussed later, getting out of the house every once in a while is good for those of us who work from home. Therefore, this is as good an excuse as any. Doing a job as a sanity saver falls into the discussion of taking care of you and that will be covered in a later section.

Everyone who does work from home needs to get some fresh air and a fresh look at the outside world. Even if it is for only a few minutes, it helps out tremendously. The fresh perspective gives you the boost to keep from feeling like you are in a rut. Why not do it and get paid at the same time? There are other jobs that get you out of the house like errand person, process servers, and couriers. However, these jobs may require the added expense of being bonded and insured. These jobs are a bit more involved than delivering phone books. Make sure you check with your local laws and regulations to ensure that these jobs do not require a business license or other requirements. The phone book delivery job is generally straightforward and requires nothing more than a license and insured vehicle. The phone book staff will advise of the requirements for your area.

I did phone book delivery two different years and received about $200 total during the delivery weeks that I worked. I did neighborhoods that I was familiar with. That helped getting the job done but the phone book staff does provide you with a suggested route. Delivery is physically demanding work because you have to get in and out of the car to deliver your phone books. Some phone companies want them at the door while others want them at the mailboxes. Be mindful that you are doing a job and they do random follow up checks before paying you. Their follow up checks involve calling telephone book customers to ensure they received their phone book in a timely manner. Alternatively, they may ride through the neighborhoods to ensure proper delivery methods. For those that have requested more than one, they check whether or not the proper amount was delivered. This is to ensure you are following the protocols as they were laid out to you. Should the phone book staff discover you did any portion of the job incorrectly, you may have to redo the route to get paid or they may dock you for the numbers of books they discover have been delivered improperly. As with any work, do the job as it is laid out and you should get your pay without delay.

While this is not a career choice it is something that can be done for some spare change during the spring of the year. There are other opportunities that come up like this. Those who want to work sporadically or every now and then are a good fit for this kind of work. It is also great if you need to save up for some extraneous expense outside of your budget. Either way, these opportunities are out there and can be a rewarding experience for the right person. While not bill payers, they also provide work experience for those that are new in the job market or are going back to work after a long hiatus from not working at all. They can also become resume builders as some contract companies will allow you to put a supervisors' number down as a reference.

Surveys

Surveys are a good way to sit at the computer all day offering up your opinions. It is an easy to earn free stuff and a little pocket change. However, it will not get you rich or pay a substantial part of your bills. I find I can do these in my spare time and it helps with my beloved "soda money."[3] Surveys also afford you the opportunity to try

---

[3] I absolutely have to have a soda next to me almost 24 hours a day. Like those that go to Starbucks every morning, it can become an expensive habit. Doing surveys provides me with the extra money each month that I can use to purchase soda and I don't have to worry about spending my wages earned from my

stuff that you would not normally try. With surveys, there is not much control over the pay. It ranges from a sweepstakes entry to $200.00. The higher paying surveys are sporadic and there is no guarantee that you will be invited to participate. Further, the higher paid shops that are generally above $4.00 are few and far between. Most pay monthly or require you to amass a certain dollar amount before "cashing out"[4] the funds in your survey account.

While this reference is made to paid surveys, there are quite a few that will let you try a product for free or at a greatly reduced price. Some of the product trial surveys will even pay you a nominal fee for the survey once you have completed the trial and follow up questions.

The most I have ever made from a survey was $150.00. This was for posting to a discussion board over a period of four weeks. While I have been invited to surveys for up to $400.00 but, I have not qualified for those for one reason or another. With product surveys, I have tried things from women's products, cereal, to game systems and new products or even television shows being considered for market. You simply try the product then share your opinion in the follow up surveys they provide. Then, you either return the unused portion to get paid or keep the product you were sent to try. As mentioned before, you have to qualify by taking a screener and then

---

traditional full-time job.

[4] Cashing out means that you have to reach a certain dollar amount then request a check in the dollar amount. The positive to this is that you can leave the earnings in your survey account and cash it in when it is worth it I normally wait until it reaches $25.00 or more. I have received a check that I requested for cash out at $57.00. It did take a while but it was a nice lunch when I finally received my check. Still, others will pay you via PayPal.

successfully complete the survey to be considered for pay. Again, this is not necessarily a moneymaker, but it is nice for earning extra pocket change. You may also qualify for gift cards to popular online shopping places. These are nice, because it affords the opportunity to shop at places I do not normally go to.

Mystery Shopping

Mystery shopping is another area of work that can be done for pocket change. There are some people who make a career out of mystery shopping but that would mean a lot of fieldwork and registration to official listings. The registration is to get the preferred shops that pay more than conventional shops. Often, registration for the preferred listings is through a preferred shopping network and there is an annual fee. These networks are like professional associations within the mystery shopping network.

When I mention fieldwork that means a lot of site visits, interaction with associates, picture taking, and filling out shop forms. For the shops that pay higher, that is ok. But some shops will pay as little as $4.00 plus a nominal reimbursement. This is not very lucrative. All shops will start out with a lower pay then, as the time draws near for the shop to be completed, the pay may go up if there has not been a shopper assigned to the specific time required to complete said shop. You can get lucky waiting for the pay to go up and you can also end up sitting around twiddling your thumbs waiting for a shop to reach a certain dollar amount.

You have to be good with scheduling and time management if you are signing up for more than one shop. You can schedule as many shops as you think you can handle but you also have to keep in mind that you have to have time to complete the shop forms and upload any necessary documents to complete the assignment. Each mystery shop has specific requirements that must be met including but not limited to certification, time frames, amount of time spent at the location and shop reports to complete. While most of the reports are done from the comfort of your own home, the shops themselves may require an on-site visit, a phone call, or a mixture of both. Jobs like this require attention to detail, transportation, an Internet connection and other requirements. Equipment like a digital camera or smart phone may also be necessary. Further, you may be required to make a purchase of which you may be reimbursed whole or in part. Pay attention to the requirements of both the company and the shops you sign up for to ensure that you are able and willing to accept the terms of the assignment. You may even be required to invest in a scanner, printer, or fax machine. Some companies will also ask that you keep your shop records on file for up to a year. This would require the purchase of a file cabinet. Locking file cabinets are preferred for security reasons. Being a mystery shopper may not be a full time job or pay the bills but it does give great work experience as well as some extra money. Then again, it is fun and can get you out of the house. Like phone book delivery, it proves beneficial if you are a true WAH Professional. Sometimes mystery shops can be done to go gift shopping. This reduces the amount you would normally pay for a gift and you get paid to shop for it. It also enables you to look for things that are outside of the normal places you go gift shopping. You can even do mystery shops for a date night. Imagine going out with your significant other to a new place and have a wonderful evening. To top it off, you get paid to go as well as reimbursed for all or part of your meal/drink purchases.

The things you are asked to do or shop for vary. Below are some examples of the things you may be asked to do while on a mystery shop:

- Describe the condition of shopping areas, bathrooms, surrounding areas and associates.
- Names of the employees you interact with.
- Whether or not employees have specific uniform items.
- Time in line or how long it took for someone to greet you.
- Note details about specific things (counters, floors, menu boards, etc.)
- Visit certain sections of the store or restaurant.
- Receipts.
- Pictures.
- Temperature, quality and flavor checks.
- Other observations and items similar to that mentioned above.

Once you complete the mystery shop, you go home and fill out a report online and submit any additional documentation such as receipts, pictures, etc. Generally, the more detailed the shop and report, the more the shop payment and reimbursement is. You usually watch a training video and take a qualification test before signing up for specific shops. This ensures that you know what the requirements are for the mystery shop. It shows that you know what you need to accomplish before starting the job and getting paid. Once you pass the qualification tests, you can sign up for subsequent shops with the same client[5] more than once without taking additional training. Normally, the only time you do additional training for the same client is if the shop requirements change or something has been added to the shop itself. Most companies will let you do multiple shops for the same client or do the same shop multiple months in a row.

As mentioned before, there are professional associations you can join to get preferred or higher paying shops. These are organizations that you can join to be considered a "gold" or "silver" shopper. With many mystery shop sites, certification qualifies you for higher shop fees and it also ensures that you have been certified as a mystery shopper. While it is nice to be a part of these organizations, it is not required for most mystery shopping companies. I personally never joined such organizations and have successfully completed shops that have ranged in pay from $4.75 to $200.00. I only did the $200.00 shop one time and I got a reimbursement pay of $175 for shopping for jewelry. I got some nice jewelry for next to nothing. I was even allowed to keep the jewelry.

Alternatively, some jobs may require a purchase and return of a specific item. Therefore, please keep in mind the requirements of the shop or you may not get paid or reimbursed and you will have wasted your time trying. Not meeting the shop requirements may prevent you from

---

[5] Client-the company that hires outsourcing companies to handle customer service/tech support/billing functions via telephone, chat, and shopping. While some companies will have their own departments, you will find that many companies will hire a third party company to hire remote agents and manage customer service aspect of business operations as well as mystery shops. Hiring outside of the company for mystery shops ensures a valid 3rd party or customer point of view.

asking for shops for this client or with the company in the future. Keen attention to detail is important with any mystery shopping venture.

On the opposite end of the pay spectrum, the $4.75 shop fee was paid for a fast food mystery shop. I was also reimbursed $6.00 for my food purchase. This is a cheap lunch date if you are treating. As mentioned before, while you may sign up for multiple shops and with multiple companies, you may be required to keep your shop documents on file for up to a year. Also, if you make more than a couple hundred dollars, you may have to pay your own taxes on the shop fees earned. Be sure to check your federal, state, and local requirements for self-employed earnings so that you do not end up owing taxes when you file your taxes at tax time.

Writing

Anyone who is familiar with the internet knows there are an abundance of writers and bloggers. Many of whom get paid for their submissions or are career journalists. While I have not done this professionally, this book is my first venture into the writing arena. There are self-publishers, bloggers, journalists, reviewers, editors, website writers and those that write via email and chat support. There are other job opportunities that use a writers skills and this can be lucrative for the right person.

Writing is a skill and good grammar and typing skills are required should you want to do this as a career. Just like trying out for the theater, the writing skills you possess are tried out by prospective employers by means of grammar tests and submissions. Anyone who has tried to become published knows the submission process well. It is a hit or miss thing and you may have to submit something to several companies or several things to one company. All of that is done before you are considered for the writing job or considered for publishing.

In this electronic world, the competition is tough because more people have access to publishers than they did before. Before the Internet, one would have to submit a paper manuscript or sample to a publisher and hope that it would be read by the editor and considered. The Internet has brought us many more editors and publishers as there are companies that publish digitally.

> Writing from home is slightly different in that you are paid either by the word or submission. Further, there are royalties and intellectual rights to be considered and you may have to do a lot more work than you want to in order to be successful. Further, do your research on the companies you are submitting your work to. Writers write from their hearts and it can be a great disappointment to submit something that is refused by a company but the submission terms dictate that you cannot submit it to another company for publication consideration.

Word of mouth organizations

Did I tell you about this great product I was given the opportunity to try[6]? Word of mouth companies are ways that products are advertised and tried and then reports are generated by the conversations you have about the products. Many word of mouth companies have a list of reps that try products out for a time period then spread the word about how great the product is. This is one of my favorite programs. While it is not a paying gig, I have been able to try many new and current products I would not normally try for free or at a greatly reduced price.

During the trial period, you complete activities like write reports about word of mouth conversations, social media mentions of the products you are trying and reviews of the products. You earn rewards on a paid or point system and can redeem the points to donate to charity, gift cards, or to use in future product trials. You also answer surveys and polls for the points. These surveys also qualify you for future product trials. There are over 75 vendors on one trial site for which you can redeem your points.

For the most part, these programs enable you to get free stuff and gift cards to your favorite retailers. Free is great if there are no strings attached. The bottom line is, everyone talks about his or her products and every Internet user has shopped online at least once. Why not get rewarded for it? Some of the things I have tried as a product trial associate are air fresheners, new food items, and an alternative game system. While the smaller items

---

[6] Word of mouth companies that allow you to earn points for spreading the word about products agents are given the opportunity to try. While not paid, it is lots of fun.

come with a coupon for one free of the item and several for up to three dollars off, others are for a nominal fee that is way below the retail value of the item. For example, the game system cost me only $49.00 when it retails for almost $200. I earned my points by spreading the word of mouth and have received $10-$100 gift cards depending on the number of points I redeemed through the redeem feature. I have also donated my points to my favorite charities for them to use to redeem for gift cards from retailers that they can benefit from. No matter how you do it, you spread the word about your favorite products. You interact with others and, as with word of mouth, it spreads free advertising for the company and product. That company gets valuable feedback from you as the trial associate and you get to try something for free or at a greatly reduced cost. It is a win-win.

Lifestyle

Working from home takes a special kind of personality. That personality combined with a certain commitment to the job and its requirements can make for a satisfying career choice. While it may sound easy or simple, it is certainly not. It is definitely a lifestyle and may require some change in order for you to acclimate to it. This lifestyle is different than any other you may encounter. A little dedication, hard work, and adjustment are necessary to make it a rewarding experience. As noted before, WAH jobs are not for everyone and you need to give it some serious consideration. It may even take some getting used to. I advise giving it at least six months' worth of trying before you decide whether or not it is the right career path for you. Any change is difficult at first but once you are used to it, you may not want it any other way.

Initially, I had to make a lot of changes in my lifestyle before this worked for me. For this last round of work, I had to change my internet service provider, rearrange my entire house, and coax my family to support me. The latter part was the hardest because they did not know how to accept that I was just in the next room and they could not bother me while I was working. However, it was a learning process and after we adjusted, it is like I have worked from home my entire life. (Well, in the kids mind, at least theirs.)

Most of the work at home jobs that actually pay an hourly or contract wage have very strict requirements for their work staff. These requirements are not set to be overly picky or exclude certain people. They just need to satisfy the requirements of the systems they use. Also, the companies want agents to come across to customers as professional. The companies do not want to have a customer call in for assistance and hear children or a barking dog in the background. Further, they do not want someone who is going to eat while working with customers or become distracted by the television or others in the room. Finally, they may not want you to let the customers know that you are working from home.

More people work from home than you think and there are more companies that hire remote agents than you may realize. When I started working customer service from home, I began to network with other customer service work at home agents and when we would discuss where we had worked before, I discovered that many of the companies I deal with have agents that work from home. From power companies, to tech support, the opportunities are endless. With the success of some of these programs, others opting for remote agents for certain areas of their customer service or tech support needs.

O.o (Work at home people all over the country.)

The real WAH jobs

Let's get to the real reason you have picked up this book. You want to work from home and you are looking for something that is truly going to pay the bills. You want to earn a wage or you may not be able to work outside of the home for one reason or another and you still want to do something other than remain in front of the television every day. Here we begin our search for a real work at home job.

Remember, this is a lifestyle and there may be things asked of you that you would not normally do in the course of your career. It is not every day that a company will ask you to run a system check to ensure hardware capability or the request of having an I9 form notarized instead of filled out with the employer. There are also basic contracts that you should be aware that you are looking at and signing. Always read everything you sign as well as ask lots of questions. There are people available to assist you with every step of the way so do not feel like you are lost in this journey. Also, if something does not feel right or sounds too good to be true, then it probably is.

From the beginning of the job search through the actual working of the job and receiving your paycheck, we are going to discuss some of the highlights and discuss what should happen along the way. While not all inclusive, the rest of this book is going to give you a good idea of what to look for and what to expect when becoming a true WAH Professional.

Search and interviews

At a bare minimum, you need a quiet place to work and an Internet connection. Some companies will require that you test your connection speed and computer components to ensure that you have the minimum acceptable services and hardware capable to do the job. Once that hurdle is passed, some may have you answer screening questions to see what job type is the best fit. Of course there is the typical application and resume submission followed by interviews. These interviews are either over the phone or via a video chat service. Both your application and resume are submitted online. The system testing, job testing, and document submissions are all typically done before you receive a response from the company advising that your information was received. This is followed by a call asking for an interview. Depending on the company, you are then requested to do additional assessments of skill or are invited to interview. Most interviews are one on one while others can be group interviews where they give everyone an overview of what the jobs entail then take those who are interested aside and perform the first individual interviews. Group interviews can take place in meeting programs using group-meeting software that is likely used on the job. These group meeting software programs will be discussed in another section later in the book.

When you finally reach this point, you have gotten someone's attention that believes you may be qualified. You are now on your way to securing your work at home (WAH) job. Be mindful that this step can take anywhere from a few days to a month or more. Patience pays off when you reach this stage. While it is not expected that you to wait for a response from every single application you send off, do submit multiple applications/resumes. Then, accept the invitations to interview as they come. The more experience you have with the process, the better you can be at it. Besides, the first offer to interview may not be fruitful but, by the time you get to the job that you think you may really want, you will have the WAH interview process down pat and you may score the WAH job of your dreams.

Often, you will receive a generic email response stating that your application has been received and that someone will be in contact with you after reviewing your qualifications. They also want to ensure that your skills meet the requirements of the job. Do not be offended if you do not get a "thanks, but no thanks" response if they decide to hire someone else. This does not reflect on anything you have done, it just means that someone else's skills more closely met the requirements of the job.

If you get past the aforementioned steps, you are either asked for a second interview or (tentatively) offered the job. The next steps are up to you. This is especially important if you are offered work. Some companies will require a background check or a drug screen. Of the companies that require a drug screen or background check, most will pay for these and advise you to take paperwork to a specific local establishment. However, there are others which may ask you to pay for them. The great thing about paying for the check is that you get a copy of the background check sent to you. You can keep a copy of the results to proactively present to future employment prospects. It is ok to be weary of this. If you are unsure about the company you are authorizing for the checks or paying to get them done, do the same legwork you did to check up on the companies you considered when starting your job search. As always, you can never be too careful. If there is a contact number or email for the potential employer, you can always call them with any questions or concerns you have. They will understand wanting to be careful with your personal information. They will be more than happy to provide you with answers to questions you ask and help you make an informed choice. If you cannot afford the fee for the background check or the timeframe for completing things like the drug screen is not compatible with your schedule, let the potential employer know. That way, they may reschedule or keep your application on file for a different position. Another job may come available at a later date that may be more cohesive with the schedule you have. This keeps the line of communication open between you and that employer and if you need to apply in the future, they will not disregard your application due to failure to complete required pre-employment screening. It also looks good if you are considered for future employment because they can look in your file and see that you attempted to keep them informed of your situation. You also explained to them that your availability was not compatible with their needs at the time. I had one such company ask me what hours I was looking for. I was not available at the times they had been hiring for but they did call me back a week later to inform me that the hours I was willing to work had become available for a job they were hiring for. At that point, they asked if I wanted one of the first interviews for that job. Gladly, I accepted. Because I kept the lines of communication open with them, they actually came back to me. That impressed me and my open and honest communication with them must have impressed them because they did call me back. Being safe with your personal information when it comes to background checks is always important. Further, keeping open lines of communication with potential employers is vital to your success and future as a WAH Professional.

On boarding

Once you pass your final interview and initial checks, you will be sent a welcome pack. This will include your formal job offer. Welcome packs will be sent to you via email, postal mail, or FedEx. Welcome packs contain many documents that you should read carefully and keep on file. It cannot be stressed enough that you need to read each and every document enclosed because it affects not only your pocket, your responsibilities as a WAH Professional and an employee. It also outlines rules and requirements as it relates to your career both with the company and after being employed by them. Finally, it has timelines for milestones that are required before starting day one of training.

This section will discuss a lot of the documents you will encounter in these packages but it is not limited to this list. Each company has their own set of documents that their employees are required to sign. The content of these documents will vary by state and local rules. This section is meant to be general and not all-inclusive.

There will be documents that you fill out with your name, address, phone number, emergency contacts, etc. While this seems redundant, even traditional brick and mortar[7] jobs will ask you to do this for their respective filing systems. It may seem silly to provide for an emergency contact, but it is still important. I once trained someone who was disabled and had a seizure disorder. Upon taking her first call, she went into a seizure. The company we worked for dictated that no one should be in your home office while working.[8] Were it not for the emergency contact information she provided I would not have been able to let her spouse know she had had a seizure. Because I notified him, he was able to go into her office, remove her headset and provide her the assistance she needed as a result of the medical emergency she experienced. Should there be any questions about what you need to provide for your employee file, please refer to your respective Human Resources personnel and they will be happy to answer those questions for you.

In the document with your personal contact information, you will find the basic job offer. This document will tell you the hours of training and production, rate of pay and other pertinent information that you may need for completion of your new hire file.

Other documents that you will encounter with every employer are the typical tax documents such as W-4, I-9, and local tax documents. These will have to be filled out and probably notarized so that the employer meets state and federal employee documentation requirements. Each company has different procedures on how to get these

---

[7] Brick and mortar- for the purposes of this text, this phrase refers to jobs that are situated in a building. WAH Professionals work in their homes, most made of wood. Therefore, buildings made of brick and mortar house businesses like call centers.

[8] This was to ensure the private information of the clients' customers as we dealt with billing issues and often had information such as social security numbers and payment method information on our screens.

filled out and submitted. There may be a notary document enclosed for you to send in with the tax documents. This is to ensure the correct amount of taxes will be taken out and reported properly to the IRS and other tax entities. Follow instructions provided when filling out and returning these to the employer. Failure to do so may delay your start date. This delay can also revoke your job offer if these documents are not returned in a timely manner.

      One document that you will encounter with most every WAH job is the non-disclosure agreement. This document will vary with each job. It is dependent on the company you work for as well as the client for which you will be working with. Non-disclosure can be as simple as only stating that you work for Company X when your client is Y. This non-disclosure asks that you keep the fact that you work for Client Y a secret. However, there are ways you can state what you do for your job without letting anyone know that you are working for client Y. For example, you work for client X doing technical support for telecommunications client Y. In your social media account you can put: "Works at Company X doing telecommunications technical support." This statement achieves non-disclosure without revealing that you work at home for Client Y. Other non-disclosure agreements may be more restrictive even to the point that if you create something that is profitable during employment with your company that the company retains all rights to said creations upon your termination of employment. You have to fully understand the entirety of the non-disclosure agreement. There is one company whose non-disclosure agreement specifically states that you cannot announce in a public forum where you work for. Public forums refer to gatherings, social media, etc. This means that the non-disclosure document should be read carefully and fully understood before signing. As always, refer to your HR representative for any questions or concerns regarding non-disclosure.

     Non-disclosure agreements are often followed by non-compete agreements. Non-compete agreements, put simply, are agreements that you will not work for another company that is in direct competition with the client or company you are working for. Some companies will even require that you tell them of all other jobs that you will be working while employed so they can make a determination about whether or not it is in direct competition with their clients' interests. Others will go so far as to require that you do not work other jobs as to not interfere with the work for which you are hired. This is important because if you fail to adhere to the non-compete agreement, you stand to lose your job as well as face any repercussions laid out in the agreement. These agreements should be taken seriously and considered as a contract. In law, breech of contract[9] could result in harsher punishments than simply losing your job. There could be fines imposed if there is found to be a breech.

     If your company is providing equipment or other resources, they will also provide you with documentation of said items and their proper use. This documentation will also cover proper care and return of the equipment in the event that employment is terminated. Physical equipment will remain the property of the employer unless

---

[9] Breech of contract-failure to adhere to a signed agreement that is within the confines of the law. Breech could result in litigation and fines if heard in court. Not all non-compete agreements have such a litigation clause but read carefully so you are aware of your rights.

otherwise stated. Your last check could be held until proper return of these items occurs. You are responsible for the care and protection of any company property you use during the course of your employment. Company property should be regarded with the same care as you would when working in a traditional brick and mortar setting.

Other documents you may encounter are specific to the company/client providing them. They are also specific to the job and all documents in your package should be read and understood thoroughly. It cannot be emphasized enough to completely understand the documents you are signing. While vital to understanding the job you are considering, reading all of the provided documents thoroughly is a good life habit. This ensures you know completely what you are getting into. By putting your signature on a piece of paper that could directly impact your actions going forward, you want to exercise great care. Your actions going forward are affected by the signed documents. It cannot be stated enough that if there are questions, always ask. The terms need to be clear and fully understood. You do not want to be caught facing consequences for something you were not aware was prohibited by the document you signed.

There may also be documents for your direct deposit. Most WAH Professionals find this to be one of the most important documents because everyone wants to get paid for their work. If you do not have an account to use for direct deposit there is paper check or pay card options provided as alternatives. Be certain that you also provide any required documents from your bank to ensure that your direct deposit will be accepted. For example, my bank has a document that you must fill out and send to them to give the company approval to put a direct deposit into your account. Failure to provide this document to them will result in the direct deposit being delayed and you may not get paid on time. This can also result in a lot of going back and forth between your employer and the bank before you get your pay check.

Finally, there will be a timeline included. Each step of the on boarding process is allotted a timeframe to enable all new employees to get their documents in before starting work. This step is required before you can start training for the job. Keep this timeline in mind when you are completing the documentation. It takes time to read the documents and have them notarized. This timeline is not impossible but may be very short. Upon receiving the on boarding package, the company wants you to start work as soon as possible. Begin working on the completion of the new hire package quickly as it is vitally important. Should you fail to meet the deadline to return the completed package, the offer of employment may be revoked. You will also have notification when your first day of work should be. This will be day one of training. Take note of this date because you may need to obtain a different headset, thumb drive, or other items necessary for the job.

Training and equipment

Upon successfully returning your new hire package and there are not any issues with it that you have to correct, it is time to go shopping. There may be items you need before starting day one of training. If you do not have the required items handy, you need to make an effort to go get them. This is where each job becomes different.

Some companies require plain old telephone service[10] others will allow for the more common VOIP[11] service. Still, other companies will allow you to use your cell phone for training or meetings. Unless you have an unlimited talk plan or long distance feature, using a cell phone is not a feasible option when training or attending meetings within the scope of your job. This is because training and meetings are done mostly on the phone and often require dialing a long distance or toll free number. Without the long distance feature, some phone services will not work. Check with your service provider for affordable options.

During training, you may be on the phone with your training group or class on a "bridge." A bridge is like a party line where everyone is on the phone at the same time. This is where a mute button will be beneficial. The trainers will ask for some sort of mute to eliminate any distractions and background noise during training. Similarly, a special phone with a wired headset may be required. Keep in mind these companies want to keep the customers information secure and a wireless headset may be against company policy. This means that a really nice $200 wireless headset is junk for your job when the $20 wired one meets all the requirements. Further, there are companies that require other items or will ship you said items via UPS or FedEx. Should they send you any equipment be sure to follow the instructions provided for

---

[10] Plain old telephone service or POTS is traditional telephone service using telephone jacks and standard lines coming into the home. While not as common as VOIP (voice over Internet protocol) service, it is available. Make sure you obtain the correct phone service, as it is vital to your job.

[11] VOIP-voice over Internet protocol. This service uses Internet signals for phone service and many companies will tell you that it does not have as a secure or reliable signal as POTS services.

set up and use. You will also note that the set up and use of company equipment may be stipulated in your new hire package as well. A few companies care about the health and well-being of their employees so they may dictate a specific set up of your home office. This is verified by providing a picture of your office or (rarely) a home visit.

While there are many variations of items available for purchase, no matter how nice, be sure to stay within the required guidelines. Going outside of requirements could result in wasting time and money on gadgets that are not compatible with work systems and you may have to miss vital information in the early days of training to go and purchase the required hardware.

There are reasons for specifics and that should be taken into account when you are shopping for equipment for your job. Nothing is more frustrating to your trainer and co-workers than to have to take extra time to troubleshoot a non-standard piece of equipment. The situation becomes more difficult for everyone involved when you have to miss training time to go to the store and install the new hardware. The trainer has to take extra time to advise you on what was missed as well as make your co-workers wait while the trainer does this. This frivolous delay in training could result in you not achieving milestones during the training process. This could result in dismissal from your job. Simply following stated requirements from the beginning is the easiest way to ensure that your employer knows you are serious about your job. This enables the trainers to make the training process as streamlined as possible. Following directions also makes things easier for all parties involved. Training moves fast and delays can cause important information to be missed. This will be discussed in more detail in another section.

Assuming you sent in your paperwork on time, purchased required items, and passed all pre-employment checks; it is time to wait for Day One of training. Training times vary and about 95% of the legitimate jobs out there will pay you for training. Length of training will vary per company and can range from a couple hours or go as long as nine weeks. Some programs will provide you with a training guide to read on your own time while other will set aside a set time for you to read the training guide. Training may consist of videos, electronic modules, interactive activities, virtual classroom and group activities. There may be other things to help you learn the aspects of the job that will be done during training. Most of these are targeted toward the adult learner and can be quite fun.

Most companies require checkpoints or tests throughout the training process. Do not stress too much about these "opportunities." These opportunities are based on information given by the trainers and require a passing grade of 80% or better. The positive side to these opportunities is that they are open book and open resource. The only requirement is that you cannot talk to your co-workers for solutions to the questions. This is designed to ensure that you know where to look on your own for answers when doing the job. There will be many tools available to you for solutions to issues that customers may call in about. These are the tools you use in your job. They are the ones that you should get the correct answers from. Knowing the policies and procedures enables you to do your job well. The checkpoints ensure that you are retaining the proper information presented to you during training.

Training is easy. You learn about the job and the company and if you are paying close attention (just like in school) to what is presented, then you will do well. You will be able to proceed to the next step of becoming a WAH Professional. Normally, the first day of training is set aside to ensure that all technical issues are taken care of before the job begins. Often, there are computer issues or hardware and ISP issues that come up and can be resolved with the companies help desk. It also enables the trainer to determine if you have purchased the proper hardware and note any missing shipments of equipment. The first day or so is often referred to as Tech Day and is for your benefit. You may or may not "work" the entire day during Tech Day. Be prepared to have your systems tested and provide information about your ISP and phone services if required.

Remember, most work at home jobs require a quiet, distraction free background. This means no kids, dogs, televisions, radios, phones, etc. in the room while you are working. Generally, a dedicated work area with a closing door can achieve this. Most WAH Professionals have an office or their workstation is in a spare bedroom or walk in closet. It is a common misconception that your kids can stay with you while working. They are a big distraction and it is not like you can get up and walk around and do other things while working with customers. This is also perceived as a security risk as you are working with customers' confidential information. How would you feel if you knew that people outside the company you were calling had access to things like your social security number and credit card information? Keeping people out of your work area during the work day eliminates any security risks. It also ensures that the clients' and customers' information are protected. If you have children you may still need a baby sitter to watch your kids while working. Even though you get the luxury of checking on them when you take breaks and lunches, they are not work place compatible and need to be kept away from your home office area while on the clock. Quiet and distraction free means just that. If there is a lot of background noise detected on your phone while training or in production, you will likely be terminated. Companies have a way of detecting which end of the phones specific noise comes from. Therefore, be aware that companies do have monitoring software that can detect if a noise is coming from your phone or from that of the customer.

 Eating while working should be limited to breaks and lunches. I have witnessed occasions where a co-worker was crunching on some chips while in a meeting and everyone in attendance heard it. This is unprofessional and rude. If there are health concerns that require you to eat every couple of hours, talk to your supervisor or trainer and they can make reasonable accommodations for you or just mute when you are eating. You do not want to eat while talking to customers either. While possible to take a bite during a lag in between calls or on a slow day, it is not recommended. This is because you do not want to sound like you are eating when a call comes in. Further, having a cup of coffee or other beverage nearby is ok. Just remember to remain professional and not gulp or slurp it loudly and try to sip only in between talking to customers. If you have to take a sip or two during a call, please use your mute button as you would when sneezing or coughing. Your mute button can be your friend so long as you use it responsibly. Most companies provide training on the proper use of using the mute button. This training provides extremely helpful in your day-to-day life as well. Even when interacting with others on the phone.

Attendance to training cannot be stressed enough. As mentioned before, the pace is quite fast as there is a lot of material to cover in a short time. This 100% required attendance in training is not meant to deter you. You can miss out on a lot and making mistakes like missing training time makes for a bad first impression as an employee. You are still trying to show your new company that you can be an asset to their work force. You want to show them that you can be dependable. You want the company to know you have a strong work ethic.

Missing work (especially during training) not only gives the appearance of not caring about your job, it causes confusion when you return. This is certainly true if you missed a lot of information presented by the trainer in your absence. You will likely have to review missed information on your own time. You also miss out on any clarification or insight that the trainer provided during the time you missed. Clarification provided by the trainer and questions asked by co-workers are beneficial during testing time. Being present during training is the easy part. It also makes the opportunities easier because you did not miss valuable instruction time. Often, the answers are provided to you during training or the associated activities. As mentioned before, these opportunities are open resource. This means you can use your personal notes, training modules, and the tools you use during the course of your job to figure out the answers. You can even ask your trainer for clarification as they are waiting for you to ask questions. With all of these resources available, it is pretty easy to make a passing grade of 80% or better. Understand that sometimes material will not be easy for everyone and these opportunities are designed to help you learn whether or not this is the right job for you.

Retakes for opportunities differ per program and while they may be available, they are not always allowed. I had one company dismiss me after the final opportunity during training simply because of a 78. There was not a retake allowed for the final and I had to find other employment. Do not let situations like that devastate you. Look at them as a learning experience. You know what you did to fall below expectations and there may be a better opportunity out there for you. If retakes are available, be prepared to come in early the next day or take it later. This is a cooling off period and provides you the opportunity to review the tested material again before taking the second try. Check with your trainer regarding retake policies for your company. It has been my experiences that there are retakes for the first opportunity but subsequent ones are pass or fail. Be aware that all companies differ on this policy.

While in training and studying for these opportunities do not allow you to get lazy and over confidant. Always keep yourself well prepared. After taking the first opportunity you know what to expect and you can adjust your learning style accordingly. As a general rule, you should take notes on any test questions that were difficult. Finding where the right answers can be found is beneficial as well. It is highly likely you will see these questions again. The last opportunity before production may be cumulative and you want to be prepared to answer most of those questions again. It is better to be prepared then caught off guard.

Once you successfully get through the training phase of your new job, you will either do some mock calls with coworkers or coaches or you will be put into the training phase of production. This is the first glimpse of what your job will truly be like. This is referred to as the nesting phase[12]. Look at it like getting settled into doing your work. It is your new virtual office and job. Mock calls may be in order before you can go to nesting. Passing the mock calls are important. For call center or sales work, a mock call is where you pretend to take a live call from a trainer/coach. They use real scenarios and the most common ones that you will encounter in the course of your employment. Mock calls apply the information you have learned throughout training in a simulated environment. It gauges your strengths and weaknesses and helps the management staff to determine if you are ready to take live calls. It also lets them know if you need more instruction. Should more instruction be needed, they coach you on the weaknesses and let you know the areas you did well in. Try to work on the weaknesses and continue the strengths. It also gives you the first opportunity to see how Quality Assurance grades the calls.[13] This grading opportunity is where a lot of your call metrics[14] come from. Call Metrics and QA grades are discussed later.

---

[12] Nesting is often referred to the highly supported production phase that is right after training. You are talking with live customers but have more support and help available then employees who have been doing the job for a month or more.

[13] Quality Assurance group is a group with your company that reviews random calls of every agent and grades them on specific requirements for each call. They look for things such as branding, politeness, verification, procedures, and how the customer is treated.

[14] Call Metrics are what customer service jobs base their performance reviews and

As mentioned before, nesting is where you speak with the customers that you deal with on a daily basis. You have quite a bit of support from management and there are extra coaches available. Your trainers will be there as well. This is the last step you will take with your trainers as they will introduce you to your team leaders and you will meet the people on your team. Often, there will be a lot more of your co-workers as the training classes may be combined for the nesting phase. You are also introduced to the format of what your virtual work environment will look like everyday. These processes vary from job to job and support can range from one on one to several training groups with many coaches, supervisors, and trainers. They are all there to help you become acclimated to your work setting. Help comes in the form of virtual chat rooms and instant messenger conversations as the coaches are listening to your calls to ensure you are handling the customers' concerns according to policy. They also want to make sure you are using your tools and the knowledge you were taught in training. It is OK to be nervous before your first live call or even at mock calls. It is simple stage fright. Of course, you want to do well. You want it to be done right and you want to make a good impression. You would not have made it this far if you were not believed to be capable of doing the job. Your trainers would not put you in nesting if you were not ready for it. The next step is production. This is the job you were hired to do.

---

job procedures on. Things like calls per hour, average handle time, hold times, and talk percentage are examples of call metrics.

Let me take a moment to officially welcome you to your new Work At Home job! You are now a WAH Professional. Congratulations! ☺

Production

You have finally reached the production stage. You have successfully made it through interviews, training and, nesting. Now you will be doing the job you were hired to do. At this point, you have your schedule, expectations, and should know how you are getting paid. You are on your way of being well versed in your job and how it all works with your company and its clients. As with any job, show up when you are scheduled, work hard, and provide advanced notice of any days you may need off. At this point, it becomes like any other job. You just work from home instead of getting up, getting dressed, and commuting to work every day. There are some residuals to consider now that you are a WAH Professional. There are pros and cons you want to think about. Some are obvious while others may not be so noticeable. These residuals will be discussed throughout the rest of this book. Like mentioned before, working from home is a lifestyle and it may not be one that you are accustomed to. If this is your first time working from home, it will certainly be a change. If you embrace the change, you will flourish as a WAH Professional.

If you discover this is not for you, then, you have learned something. You have created a learning experience that has probably left an impression on you. Don't worry. You know what to expect should you decide to try again later on. Working from home is not for everyone and not all lifestyles are conducive to a successful work at home career. For those of us that can make it work, it will make or break you. Should you not try to achieve a healthy lifestyle while being a WAH Professional, it can wear you out quickly. You can also grow tired of it. Taking care of yourself and your home become more important. As you continue your career as a WAH Professional taking care of yourself and your home is just as important as the job itself. Remember, it is a lifestyle. No two people will approach it the same.

Hours

Different companies have different shifts and hours available. Make sure you find out how your hours work to ensure you are working what you are willing and available to do. Below are some examples of shifts I have worked as a WAH Professional:

o   Friday through Monday, ten-hour shifts (9 a.m. to 7 p.m. or 10 a.m. to 8 p.m.)
o   5 days a week 8 a.m. to 4 p.m. (one weekend day required, 2 days off, varied.)
o   PT hour with shifts varying from 1 hour to 12 hours. Up to 34 hours a week.
o   Split shifts (10 a.m. to 2 p.m. and 7 p.m. to 11 p.m.)
o   Or other variations of the above.

While not all inclusive, the above list is to show you that there are a variety of shifts available. You may be lucky enough to find a traditional 9-5 but do not be on the lookout for that when you first start looking for work. Some companies also offer graveyard shifts. Anything is possible.

Another thing about being a WAH Professional is the ability to pick up hours or give them away. Each company has different ways of allowing these practices and will be covered during training or your first meetings with your team leader. Also, pay attention to the hours required to qualify for benefits. Each company differs on what they require for benefits qualification purposes. Finally, when requesting time off, follow the company policy about how much advance notice you should give your scheduling team for the days you need. This includes requests for time off for appointments, vacation, family get togethers, etc. A general rule of thumb is at least two weeks. I have found it beneficial to let scheduling know as soon as I find out I need time off as well as at the two-week mark. Should there be any errors in scheduling, find out your company's scheduling policy to determine what you need to do to get errors corrected as soon as you notice them. The sooner any discrepancies are taken care of, the less difficult it is to clear them up.

Most WAH companies I have worked for use a points system for attendance[15]. Sometimes things come up and you cannot help but missing work. As long as the absence reasons are not habits, the points system can work for you. The bottom line is, be mindful of your tardies, early outs, and absences. Each of these infractions will cost you points. An accumulation of a certain amount of points can cost you your job.

---

[15] Points generally start out at 100 and are taken away for things such as tardies, hours, and shifts missed. Points can be awarded back for volunteering to come in during high volume times when you are not scheduled as well as perfect attendance or extra weekend hours worked. Each company has a different threshold that dictates when you are let go due to attendance issues. While there is some give, do not take advantage of it or your will lose points rapidly.

When you begin your workday, similar to taking the time to get to a traditional office job, you have to take time at your WAH job to "commute to work." This commute is getting your systems logged on and ready to go. This way, you can clock in at the exact time you are scheduled to work. This means that your scheduled start time is when you have to be ready and available to work. All the signing in and getting things open are taken care of beforehand. Make sure you take enough time to turn on your computer, log in, check your schedule, learning updates and ensure that you are ready. Sometimes difficulties happen. Things like Internet and power outages, computer errors, and even tool outages (very rare) can cause delays in starting on time. You will eventually get your own timing down as to how long your "commute" to work will be. Should you run into any difficulties logging in and starting on time, notify your team leader or supervisor as soon as the difficulty occurs. Also, be sure to follow company policy regarding tardies and call outs. As a rule of thumb, I like to start my commute approximately 15-30 minutes before my scheduled start time. This ensures that everything is ok. It also gives me a few extra minutes to review any material I may be having a hard time with and to make a last minute trip to the rest room. I even have time to refresh my coffee.

One final note on attendance is worth mentioning. While you are not getting paid to log into your systems, it is still part of your job to ensure you are totally ready by your start time. Often, the misconception is that you should get paid from the minute you turn on your computer. Traditional companies do not pay you from the time you get into your car, so why should work at home companies pay you for turning on your computer. Think of getting logged in as your ride in the car to work. Make your commute a successful one. Like brick and mortar jobs, if you are stuck in traffic, call your supervisor. Same goes for troubles logging in. This ensures that your job is still yours by the time you get there.

Sometimes, life will get in the way. You may have to leave early due to illness, emergency, or some other valid reason. Discuss how this affects your attendance points with your supervisor. Like being late, if something happens that prevents you from working, (i.e., power loss, system failure, etc.) immediately notify your team leader or the TLOD.[16] This ensures that it does not appear that you quit your job. An email is always a good idea so that you have documentation that you did notify your supervisor whether he was working or not. I always follow up my emails for such emergencies with a telephone call.

Alternatively, there are times when business may be slow and there will be opportunities where you can volunteer to leave early or get approval to stop talking to customers long enough to work on training updates (learning modules.) It is strongly suggested to take these early out opportunities only when necessary. Some supervisors may place limits on who can and how many early outs an employee is allowed during a specific time period. Similarly, others may not allow early outs for those employees who are not meeting their call metrics.[17]

[16] TLOD-commonly used acronym for Team Leader on Duty.

[17] Call metrics, mentioned earlier, are used to gauge how well you are doing your job. While not a competition with anyone, they are ranked and very important. If you are meeting the goals set, then you should have nothing to worry about.

Make sure that you also let your supervisor know of any volunteer offs you take advantage of. You certainly do not want them looking for you when you have been approved for a volunteer early out.

Similarly, there is the rare occasion where there are mandatory early outs. This is where the forecasts for call volume are much lower than the forecast and there are too many people working. An example would be: there are five calls coming in during the course of an hour. If there are 25 agents ready to take calls, there are a lot of agents just sitting around waiting for the phone to ring. This would cause the supervisors to make a decision to send people home early. While rare, it happens and it is not something that is going to occur for an extended period of time. It may be rough on your paycheck but, don't worry, busy times are ahead. You will make it up in time. Whether it is mandatory or voluntary, early outs affect you and if you have benefits, may affect your status to keep your benefits. Like checking your wallet, keep up with your hours worked per week. This is especially true if you do not want to lose your benefits or full time status.

The opposite of leaving early, is picking up extra hours during busy times to handle increased work volume. Referred to as jump-ons, this can provide you with extra hours or make up for time you missed by leaving early or having to take a day off for a valid reason. Each company has their own way of finding employees who want to pick up extra hours. Notification of these opportunities will vary by company. You will be told how to receive such notifications and how to pick up extra hours if you are interested. From personal phone calls, to text messages or messenger services, jump-ons are a great way to gain more experience in your job or to make some extra money. There are other perks that may be offered. During the busy season for your client, there may be incentives such as point deals, gift cards, or other gifts for volunteering outside of your schedule. Some companies will even approve overtime or extra compensation of sorts.

Expenses

Thinking about money, expenses are another item worth mentioning. Think about the money you are paying for your work at home job. Likely, you are using space in your home for your work area. Whether it is an actual office, bedroom, closet or hallway, it is your workspace. It takes electricity to power that workspace. You are also paying for your Internet and phone services. This section is not concerned with whether or not your bills increase because you work from home but just to consider the things you are using. If you have to use your own computer, the cost for that counts as well.

Now that we have considered our expenses, lets see how that can become a benefit to a WAH Professional. There are some tax benefits involved. While these benefits vary from state to state, some expenses (like the ones aforementioned) can be used as write offs at tax time. Make sure you consult your respective tax laws regarding home office write offs and expense reductions. This also goes for home office deductions as well as contract work earnings and expenses. It is also worth mentioning that there are a few companies that reimburse you for a portion of your Internet and phone services that are used within the scope of your job. This is normally listed as a benefit and you may not be eligible until after a certain time period before reimbursement occurs. Also, be aware that if you are reimbursed for these services, they may not be qualified as a deduction on your tax return. Your Human Resources personnel will be able to answer questions regarding utility reimbursement and what you qualify for.

Most of this book has been largely about customer service, chat support, or sales. Briefly covered in the early chapters were other types of work. These were mentioned in order to let you know there is other work available to the WAH Professional. Most companies that hire traditional employees[18] seek some sort of customer service professional or that you spend most of your working day interacting with customers in a service capacity. The next section will cover contract work.

Contract work

Contract work, while still technically work, is a bit different than your traditional paying jobs. Contract work is work that should be approached with caution and due diligence or situations will occur that you may not be prepared for. Generally, contract work is on an as needed basis and you must pay your own state, federal and local taxes. You can do this periodically or when you file at tax time. Contract work also involves different forms than you are used to. These forms are beyond traditional W-2's one gets when working a job that takes out taxes from your paycheck.

---

[18] Traditional employees, for this purpose, are those that receive a paycheck with taxes and deductions taken out.

It is a true testament to one's ability to set aside money and save it. The purpose of saving is two-fold. One, you have to pay the taxes you owe on your earnings. You have to pay these taxes no matter what. The earnings are reported to the IRS and there is no way around this responsibility. You want to make sure you are setting aside enough money because you do not want to be caught with a shortfall. Paying your taxes periodically or quarterly is a better idea than to wait and do it annually so that if you do come up short, it will not be such a large burden on your pocket. This periodic payment schedule also breaks the payment up into manageable chunks so you won't be so tempted to spend the money you see growing in the savings account. Remember to set up an account for your tax funds. This also allows you to arrive at tax season more informed and prepared for filing. Second, you want contract work to supplement your full time income and not rely on it as your only source of income. Contract work is not necessarily steady work and can be very sporadic. Once, I signed on with a company to do work for a year and worked the first two months. Then, there was no more work for me the rest of the contract year. Had I depended wholly on that job as my only source of income, I would have been in a difficult financial situation. If your full time pay check has taxes coming out of it, have them take out the maximum possible or request an extra few bucks to be taken out and paid to federal and state deductions so that your contract taxes will not be such a burden for you to deal with later. As always, keep up with your respective tax laws when dealing with situations that fall outside the traditional paycheck jobs. In the end, if there is not a return on your taxes, you can be assured that they are paid and it is one less bill that you have to be concerned with.

As stated before, contract work is on an as needed basis. Therefore, when a project is done, you have to wait until the next project comes along before working again. If you live check to check, this can put a hardship on getting your bills paid. It is certainly felt if you have to wait more than a couple of weeks for the next project to start. Contract work, if done right, can provide many benefits when supplementing your income. It is also great at filling the gaps in between the hours you work at your regular job. However, it takes dedication, patience, and attention to detail to keep you out of the tax troubles. Above all, if the WAH Company you work for is not taking out taxes, please read the laws carefully and ensure you are paying your taxes like you should. The contract company will not tell you how to do that. They will only tell you that paying taxes on your earnings is your responsibility.

Legitimacy

It is worth discussing things that you will encounter along the way in your search for the best fit. Work at home jobs are not for everyone. On the forefront of everyone's mind is the legitimacy of the job offer. You can never be too careful. Just because a job is listed in your local paper or in the unemployment office listings, does not mean that it is legitimate. When you find something you are interested in, do not be afraid to check out the legitimacy of the job. There are several ways to do this.

For companies that offer work at home (remote) as well as traditional jobs, they are certain to have a Human Resources office that you can contact with your questions. Remain polite and inquire about the things that you are unsure of. The purpose of Human Resource personnel is to answer these inquiries. Such personnel will be more than happy to go over any vague job descriptions and explain job requirements for work at home or remote agents. Some of these companies will require you to train at a local site. Be aware of these requirements because you may not be able to attend training if you have no way there or it is further than you are willing to travel. Others will do training virtually. If you find that your local telephone or power company offers work at home positions, these jobs are usually legitimate and revolve around customer service, collections, or sales. Some may even offer dispatch positions, where you communicate to their field techs.

Similarly, there are companies that are technology or e-commerce related that offer work at home opportunities. Just like the local industries that offer in-house and remote jobs, there are HR personnel you can contact to ensure that they have a legitimate business location. Also, do not be afraid to visit the main website to ensure the job posting is also mentioned on the company's official career site. (Assuming you found it on a job board or somewhere else.) There are also other resources you can utilize in order to check for legitimacy.

Finally, there are employers that are truly outsourcing companies that provide customer service, sales, and support for companies that are willing to outsource to remote agents. These are the companies that you want to make an extra effort to check up on. You can look them up by doing a simple search on the web for starters. However, do not believe everything you find in the search results and be careful what you click on in a search result listing. This simple first step will give you a grasp on how some people perceive the company you are researching. You will come across the company itself, review postings, and may even find You Tube videos. The Better Business Bureau has their own site where you can look up companies. When you visit this site, you will look for the company by name. It lists what industry, how long in business, whether or not they are BBB accredited and how old their BBB file is. The main things that are important are type, how long in business, and accreditation. If the industry matches the job type you are seeking AND they are accredited, then it is very likely that the job is not a scam. Also, the longer they have been in business, the better you should feel that it is legitimate.

      Work from home employees are not as new a concept as some people think. I have looked up companies that have "remote customer services" listed as their industry and have been in business since 1990. At this point, if you are still unsure, you can look at their Facebook, Twitter, or other social media pages. You can even find sites that people use to network as well as work from home sites. This information should quell any fears that you may have of being scammed. Finally, if you are lucky enough to find a Facebook page (for example,) ask questions on the page or of the people who are posting comments on the social media outlet. This is a great source of first-hand information. While not everyone will post positively, do not focus on one experience. Instead, take a broad look at what everyone is saying and see if it is mostly positive or negative. This will enable you to make an informed decision based upon all information gathered instead of basing your decisions on the opinion of just one person.

Scams

You can never be too careful when it comes to your pocket, time, and personal information. It is not politically incorrect to do your own background checks on a company you are thinking about working for. While there are many legitimate jobs out there, there are just as many that are sketchy. Some are outright scams. Therefore, make sure you ask lots of questions. There are also places on the web you can go for valid information about WAH jobs. From work at home job boards to websites such as Linked In, Facebook and more, there is a wealth of information out there. It is also important to network with your co-workers when you do finally start working from home. Many of them have worked for other companies and can give you some legitimate leads.

I once did some work that I felt was not legitimate. This job advertised for "virtual assistants" This entailed searching home listings for "clients" and calling the listings and obtaining information about the home listed. There was elaborate information that I had to obtain using Google Docs[19]. All of the "staff" contacts used internet phone services.[20] You made all your inquiry calls from an internet voice number. It all seemed very professional, and they did not ask for any personal information outside of their job application. What had me worried was that I only spoke with one company official the entire time. Further, they wanted me to work 20 hours unpaid. It was a "try it

---

[19] www.google.com/docs is a document sharing website where you can enable many users to manipulate the same document. This can range from excel spreadsheets to word documents and surveys.

[20] It enables the use of voicemail and phone services for professionals who do not wish to tie up or disclose their personal phones for business purposes. There are many programs available for internet phones.

out" period and if you liked the work, then you were hired. This also enabled them to determine if they liked your work or not. You entered your hours on a spreadsheet and this document was also where you clocked in and out. Everyone did their unpaid calls for a "training client" and it seemed that others were working for the same training client because you could see everyone's hours and time and places called. You scheduled your hours around the other people working and filled in time slots that were not already taken. One of the things that unsettled me was that I never seen the same name in two places. There were several places that I would have had to visit on a regular basis and common sense told me that I would see names at least more than once and I did not. Only first names were used. Further, it was also difficult at best to get hold of my supervisor. Often, it was up to 48 hours before my supervisor addressed any concerns I had. I did this for about six hours (2 hours a day over the course of three days) and decided it was not something that felt right. I just quit. I never heard from anyone about it and someone got six hours worth of effort out of me for free. Never again will I walk into something like that.

Another job that I tried and decided it did not feel right was a research job. It was an ad in the local newspaper listings that they posted on their website. I responded to the "request for more information" thing on the website and got a couple of professional looking emails from the "company" outlining the requirements and skills needed. The second email I received from this company was offering a selection of interview times. It looked legitimate. This email even went into detail about some of the great things you could do research for. In hindsight, researching surfboards or other simple things are not topics

I would pay someone to do work on. I got my appointment call and it seemed to go well. I made note of the number that the interviewer called from. They even told me to call that number should I have any questions. I let them know I would think the offer over and call them back in 48 hours. They even responded with an email noting that it was a pleasure speaking with me and they looked forward to speaking again in the future.

After thinking about the offer, I had some questions and decided to call the number. I found the person on the other end had answered with a hello instead of a professional greeting. This did not settle well with me. I simply stated that I had a wrong number and hung up. I was certain I dialed the right number. I tried again and the same voice with the same greeting. I immediately hung up. I remember thinking "Well, that was not legit." It was a good thing that I listened to my gut instinct because around 7:30 p.m. that evening, I was inundated with emails and received two calls (of which I let go to voicemail) demanding that I needed to start work soon. After a couple of weeks the emails and the calls stopped. I knew this was not how a professional company treats their employees or potential employees. This is my testament to you to validate that you should be careful and thoroughly research WAH job listings and offers.

Technical Difficulties

Your respective companies have policies regarding technical issues. In some (while very few) instances, they may give you tech pay. This can range from minimum wage to your hourly wage. If it is their equipment that fails or their servers go down, you may still get paid for your time scheduled. While rare, it does happen.

If you are using your own equipment, your Internet has an outage, the power goes out, electrical storms, etc, and then it is your dime. Not only does this prevent you from clocking in and working, it also may give you attendance points for chronic problems. Bottom line; technical issues happen. Be prepared in the event something goes wrong. While it is important to have a computer that meets your company's standards, it is nice to have a back up. In my set up, I normally have one for work as well as my back up or personal one. This way, if one fails, I still am able to work using my back up machine until I get the failed pc fixed. I also am not likely to miss any work while waiting for the fix. This may not be possible for everyone. Computers are not exactly cheap but it is strongly recommended you have a set up with at least two machines. No company will tell you that and there has never been a requirement for me to have 2 computers. It is just easier to be safe than sorry.

Extra headsets are always a plus. You never know when a headset will simply stop working or you accidentally run over the cord with your chair severing the cord. Even spilling your coffee is a possibility. While it is quite easy to run to the store and purchase a new item, you save money (by not missing work) if you have a spare handy. The same can be said with keyboards, mice, and monitors. However, if a second set up is in your office then, these items are already handy. It is also impressive when you take a few minutes to simply switch out a defective piece of equipment compared to missing a whole day going to the store and installing a new one upon your return. Finally, cables and plugs are also necessary. One can never have too many of these lying around. Ethernet cables, phone cords, and power strips do not last forever and you do not want to be stuck having to go to the store over a $2 cable when you can replace it from you back up cables. Having spares can save time and money. Every WAH Professional believes it to be a great investment. Especially if one were to go bad during a time you do not have the extra few bucks to run and replace something.

It is important to keep your utilities paid and up to date to prevent billing disconnects. Your WAH employer is not interested in hearing about your services being disconnected for nonpayment. It is your business and your responsibility to keep your bills paid. Point is, if you want your job; keep your Internet, power, and phone bills paid.

When it comes to Internet service, you want to make sure you have the required speed and services. Be prepared for outages. While it should not occur often, if at all, try to make sure it is a minimal occurrence. If you ever have to change your Internet services or change your provider, make sure you plan for a temporary interruption of your connection while everything gets changed over. I did not learn about this until I did technical support for an Internet service provider. Sometimes, when you change your service within the same ISP, your service will be temporarily disconnected while changing it from one speed to another. This is similar to moving a book in the library from one self to another. While the disconnect may be temporary, it will likely occur. These events should be planned for and done during the days you are off. If not, you miss some work. Make sure you let your supervisor know what is going on. They may be able to work something out with you and let you know if you are making a bad decision or not. They can also verify whether or not your new Internet services and speed will be compatible with your work systems. As with any major change, communication is vital. WAH companies have to do a lot of back end work to ensure you can be successful at your job. There are very valid technical reasons why you have your computer and Internet speed tested before hire. If something changes like your provider or speed, the WAH Company may have to make changes on their end to minimize difficulties upon returning to work. If possible, you may also want to give a dry run of logging in to your systems to make sure there are not technical issues upon your return to work. Also, not all computer systems are the same. If you have to get a new machine, make sure it is compatible with your work systems. I once planned for 5 months on getting the perfect machine for work. I went above and beyond to make sure it was compatible and had more than the minimum requirements for my work. This paid off because I did not have any troubles making sure my system was up to par for other companies' requirements after purchase.

Changing your phone service should also follow the same basic principals. Phone service options need to be scrutinized. Phone service types vary between companies. Generally, if a phone plugs into a standard phone jack, it is plain old telephone service.[21] There is nothing digital about it. If the power goes out, it still works. (So long as your phone is not cordless, of course.) There are also digital phones that come through the cable lines. VOIP or Voice

---

[21] Plain old telephone service-POTS-Phone service using traditional phone lines and cables and that comes via a standard phone jack from cables at the street. POTS are quite different from Internet, bonded, or fiber optic telephones.

Over Internet Protocol is one type of Internet phone. You will find that most WAH companies prefer POTS to VOIP phones, as they are more stable and secure. Finally, there is also Internet phones or Magic Jack type phones that plug into the Internet modem, computer, or standard electrical jack. Wholly unreliable, these types of phones should be avoided when considering phone service for work.

Lastly, electricity should be mentioned. Outages are not common. If a planned outage is announced for maintenance reasons, immediately let your supervisor know upon receiving notification from the power company. This way, your schedule can be adjusted accordingly. Power failures due to weather happen also. Obviously, you cannot plan for thunderstorms or other weather emergencies. Pay close attention to your local weather. You do want to be safe during electrical storms. After all, you have a headset connected to a machine with electricity going through it. If the storm is very close, notify the supervisor on duty and shut everything down. Proactively, it is better to let supervisors know that there is a storm headed your way in the event you have to get off work in a hurry. This puts the employer on notice that you need to remain safe during the storm.

Weather emergencies and evacuations are another time you need to let management know what is going on. This is why it is important to keep your supervisors' office number and the sick line number handy. During your evacuation, storm, or power failure, you can call and keep them informed of your situation. As always, communication is a virtue you cannot be without. Make sure you keep up with your company's policy regarding weather emergencies and utility outages. Double check the policy often to make sure there are no changes since the last time you reviewed the policy. This ensures you know the correct policy and can plan accordingly. Further, make sure you know what states your company operates in. Should you have to evacuate to a relatives' house and their Internet service is compatible with your companies' systems, you may be able to bring your work computer with you and still work. Make sure that you can operate for your company in the state you are evacuating to and make sure their Internet and office area is conducive to your work. It would make a good impression on your supervisors if you went out of the way to make it to work even though you are not in your home due to an evacuation.

      Should all remain well technically, you want to make sure you keep healthy and sane while you are a WAH Professional. It is important that you do not let your health slide as an at home agent. Working from home is a career choice and it is certainly a lifestyle adjustment. Especially true if you are not used to being at home a great deal. If you have never worked from home before, you will encounter challenges that are certain to make you question your career choice. This working from home thing is not the same as bringing your work home from a brick and mortar job than working at home for a couple of days. If you have a job like that this affords you the luxury of bringing your work home then, great. That is not the lifestyle change to which this refers. At the very basic level, there are things one must learn along the way. It is truly trial and error and you will eventually find what works best for you.

Breaks and Lunches

  Breaks and lunches are important. This gives you time to decompress, walk away from your desk, go to the rest room, and refill your drink. It is beneficial to get up and move around (preferably away from your desk) throughout your shift. It may seem trivial but it accomplishes a couple of things. First, it gives your eyes a rest from looking at the computer screen. It also gives your back a break from sitting for an extended period. While you can sit for hours and hours at your computer, it is healthy to change your position every now and then. This is to prevent stiffness. Sitting for extended periods puts a great deal of pressure on your back. A comfy chair will alleviate some of that pressure. Taking a break also lets you stretch for a moment and get some air. Second, decompressing from an intense work session may help you keep your cool. Finally, it is just what the names imply. It is good to take a break and you should take a lunch sometimes. It is also recommended that you reserve eating times for when you are on break or lunch. Most companies will tell you that you should not eat while working anyway. This also leads to making healthy lifestyle choices. It is all too easy to fall into the habit of snagging a bite or two between calls throughout your shift. This is not a good idea nor is it healthy. While it is strongly suggested that you not eat while on shift, keeping a drink handy is a good habit. Your preferred beverage (preferably ice water but anything will do) is great to keep you hydrated and for a sip if your throat happens to get dry or scratchy.

  Hands, legs, and back

Most work at home jobs will require lots of work using your hands. It is important to keep your hands stretched out to prevent fatigue and carpal tunnel injuries. You should also learn correct position for typing and sitting by learning a couple of things from an ergonomic[22] website or professional. Paying attention to ergonomic tips will also prevent injury. The three following exercises were taught to me at a restaurant I used to work at and have helped me a great deal.

- Wrist stretch. (Stretches inner wrist.)
    1. Extend your arm straight out in front of you, palm down.
    2. Using your other hand, pull your fingers toward you by reaching to the palm side and pulling backwards toward you.
    3. Hold for a count of fifteen.
    4. Do the same for the other side and repeat each side two more times.
- Finger extensions. (Stretches hand and fingers.)
    1. Open your hands and extend fingers as wide apart as possible.
    2. Hold for a count of ten.
    3. Close hand into a fist, hold, and then relax.
    4. Repeat for other side.
    5. Do each side two more times.
- Finger push-ups. (Strengthens fingers and wrist.)

---

[22] Ergonomics- Human engineering. The practice of setting up your work area to ensure the most comfort and least amount of injury from repetitive motions. These motions can be typing or staring at a computer screen.

1. Open hand and place finger tips on the counter. Imagine you have a tennis ball under your palm.
2. Push down with only fingertips on the table.
3. Hold for a count of 5 and repeat 2-3 more times.
4. Repeat for other hand.

These exercises should help keep your hands and wrists limber as well as assist in preventing injury. They can be done quickly and at any time during your shift. It is also recommended that you do them at other times when you are not working. There are other exercises that can be done just as easily. Do some research and find the best ones for you.

You also want to stand up and stretch or just stand up at your chair every once in a while. This helps your back and legs and prevents stiffness. I find I can do this while working. Even getting up for just a moment gives your body a chance to reset and rest from constantly sitting in your chair. There are other little exercises you can do while sitting at your desk. They can be used to prevent stiffness and fight fatigue. Some exercises easily done are ankle rotations, neck rolls, shoulder rolls, and leg rises. You do not want to remain in the same sitting position for the 8-10 hours you work everyday. It is not healthy and moving around or standing up every now and then will certainly keep you alert and prevent stiffness.

Once you decide that you really want to remain a WAH professional, it is beneficial to invest in a good desk and even better desk chair. A good desk has enough room for your computer, phone, other equipment and sufficient workspace. It will also allow your keyboard to be positioned so that you can sit and have your arms bent at a 90-degree angle while typing. This position, along with proper chair placement prevents fatigue while working. Make sure your desk is sturdy. A rocky desk is dangerous for both you and your equipment. The Internet is a good resource to check for ergonomic suggestions when looking for a good home office desk.

A good chair should have a solid back for lumbar support. It should have a 5-star base with wheels and an adjustable height. If you want arms on your desk chair, make sure the arms are adjustable or at least allow for your arms to comfortably rest at a 90 degree angle at the elbows. A chair with stationary arms may cause you to hunch your shoulders while typing or prevent you from sitting comfortably while working. Chair arms should be adjusted so that you can bend your arms at the elbow without interference. This will allow you to type properly without resting your wrists on the edge of the desk or keyboard tray. While it may be on the pricey side, a good, comfortable desk chair is essential to prevent pain and enable comfort while working. Besides, you are going to spend a great deal of time sitting in that chair. It should be comfortable. Finally, as with any home office purchase, consult your local tax laws regarding write offs for your office furniture expense.

Killing time (while keeping your sanity)

You will often encounter job descriptions that advertise back-to-back customer service calls. While that is optimal, there will be times when work is not quite back-to-back. You may encounter days where there anywhere from one to several minutes between calls. It is strongly suggested you keep your in-between call activity to reading articles pertaining to the job, there will come a time when you can step back from that and enjoy the occasional lull in the back-to-back calls. You do have the option to sit there and stare at your screen waiting for the next call or stare into space. That is your choice. You can also use this time to stand up for a minute or take a sip of your tasty beverage. However, depending on how you feel about those activities, it can make the pace of your workday slow down to a crawl. Something simple as a coloring book or a word find can help pass the time during these slow periods. You do not want anything too involved and you do want to make sure you are up to date on your work policies. First and foremost, read those work articles. Otherwise, sanity savers are something that you can put down quickly when the next task comes in. In fact, I wrote another one of my books, "Letters to My Children" as well as sections of this book in between customers.

Working in your floppy puppy slippers

One of the best perks to being a WAH professional is that you can work in your pajamas, sweat pants, or whatever. While this may sound great, it is easy to fall into a rut. It enables you to let your appearance go. Albeit tempting, still get up, brush your teeth and hair and change your clothes. There is no need for a suit and tie, but changing into fresh clothes for the day does make you feel better. Making the effort to keep up your appearance makes you feel good about yourself as well. It makes you feel better about you and the lifestyle you have chosen. When you feel good about yourself, it shows in your work. As a WAH Professional, taking care of yourself is even more important because you are not moving around as much as you would in a conventional brick and mortar job.

When you work from home, you eliminate a lot of the effort involved in getting ready. You are also eliminating the walking from your car and back. Think about it. There is the walking from your house to your car. Then there is walking from the car into the building to your workstation. Also, throughout the day you may be walking to different areas of the building. Then, at the end of the day, you walk from your workstation to your car. Finally, you walk from your car to your home and then changing clothes and settling down for the evening. That is a lot of movement your body is missing when you are a WAH professional. Less movement and walking can make you lazy. Do not let your job make you lazy. It is paramount that you make the extra effort to make up for that loss of movement as it can adversely affect your health if you don't. Even investing in a treadmill will assist is preventing laziness and help maintain a healthy lifestyle. If you do not have the money or space for a treadmill, walking around your house or actively seeking some other physical activity will pave the way for a healthy WAH career.

Sunshine

Most people take natural sunlight and fresh air for granted. Some people purposely avoid sunlight during specific times of the day or altogether. However, there are vitamins that your skin can only absorb from sunlight. You can tell you are missing those vitamins when you go outside for a few minutes and the warm rays of the sun stream down on you and it feels like heaven. It makes you want to close your eyes, turn your face to the sun and bask in its glow. It feels that good. Because I work during the day, I love to have my blinds slightly open to see the sunlight and to remind me to take a step out on the deck for a breath of fresh air. I also love to feel the warmth of the sun on my face even if just for a moment. It is almost as good as a warm towel, fresh out of the dryer, after your shower. As a WAH professional make it a point to get out of the house sometimes, move around, and get some sun once in a while. Your body and mind will thank you for it.

Human contact

You can do everything online these days. For someone who wants to be recluse, working from home makes the dream a complete package. For the rest of us, working from home makes having a normal (according to the rest of the working world) life even more important. Because your office is just in the next room, the temptation to work all the time will be ever present. Certainly it is ok to get overtime, but do not let the money make you. YOU make the money.

Make an extra effort to spend time with your family and friends. Even grocery shopping will become a treat if you work more than your standard 40 hours a week. Humans, by nature, love interaction with other humans. Virtual contact changes that interaction and can make for a lonely existence. I don't get out much during the work week but do love an excuse to get out of the house every chance I get. It makes me appreciate that we are not alone on this planet. WAH Professionals can testify that their families and non-virtual friends have an important role in their well-being. Don't let your job take you over. You have to make an effort to maintain an existence outside of your work from home career. This is part of the lifestyle.

Networking

Depending on your own social, networking, and computer skills, you will find that you will make some friends along the way. Yes, virtual friends are not technically real friends but they are a great resource. It is possible these virtual friends have worked together for a long time and are from various experiential backgrounds. Each personality is one of a kind and maybe not quite what you would find in a traditional job setting. Keep in mind; most of these people are professionals just like you. Some are a little sharper tongued than others. However, those are the ones you can learn the most from. Their wit makes you think and they keep you on your toes so that you can find the answers to your questions (most likely a procedure or an article) on your own. This enables you to be the best

WAH Professional you can be. These people and others that you befriend along the way are your greatest source of information when it comes to looking for another job. Especially true for work at home positions. You will find ways and opportunities to gather that information. This family of agents that you become part of will be your greatest asset should you decide this one job is not your perfect fit or you find yourself looking again. Maybe the contract you were working on is finished or there was a temporary layoff. You may even decide that this was not the perfect WAH job and want to seek a different position. These associates are going to provide great insight into what you should look for or even what companies are hiring. They have been in your shoes before and that extends the networking even further. If you never have to find another WAH job and the one you are currently in is the perfect fit, you can still network and help others. One day you will find the WAH job that fits you as great as those floppy puppy slippers you love so much. This is what makes you a WAH Professional. While others are finding their way, help them along. Remember, you were in their shoes once. Searching blindly in the dark for your place in the light is a lot easier when someone with an extra flashlight comes along and helps light your way.

Keeping Confidentiality

If you pay close attention to the policies and procedures of your WAH company as well as reflect upon those of brick and mortar sites, you will note there is a common theme. These employers all expect you to keep sensitive customer information confidential. Their customers will give you personal information and you confirm or even update their file. Often, the customer will have to give you the information and you simply say thank you or let them know they have verified the proper information. I have yet to find a WAH company that will ask you to read something personal back to the customer. This is done to ensure that nobody can hear the information you are confirming. This aids in protecting the customer, you, and your employer. Information you work with can include, but is not limited to, credit card numbers, names, addresses, phone numbers, and the last four of a social security number. If you are in a billing position, you may deal with even more sensitive information and you do not want someone to overhear what you are doing. This will prevent others from stealing the identity of your customer. This would be catastrophic for all parties involved should an identity theft occur.

Thinking about it from a security standpoint, it does make sense. Your family is in the next room or you may be near a window. People may be able to hear what you are doing. This is why some companies will require that your windows are shut and your office has a door that closes. Anyone outside your window or office has a potential to hear what you are doing. Therefore, follow procedures regarding personal identifiable information[23] and the security of customer accounts.

Along these same lines, be mindful of how your office is set up. Try to keep your monitor from facing windows and doors. Your face should be looking at the window and/or the main door to your office. This ensures that no one can see the computer screen should they enter or walk by. Remember, you are viewing private customer information (PII) and you do not want anyone other than you to view that information. If it is aesthetically impossible to have your computer screen facing away from all windows and doors, you can purchase a changing screen to place behind you to obstruct the view. You can also hang opaque curtains on your windows. Alternatively, you can move your office to a different location in your home.

Be aware that some companies will ask for a picture of your office to ensure that you meet space and ergonomic requirements. This is ok and is not an invasion of your privacy. This just ensures that you, as an employee, are doing everything required by the company to protect the identity of the customers as well as enforcing ergonomic policies. The bottom line is to be aware that you are dealing with sensitive information. This information could be personal or proprietary. The policies your company has are in place to protect them, the customer, the client you are working for, and you. Not revealing to your customers that you work from home goes a long way in ensuring customer confidence in the client you are working for. It also increases the reliability of the reputation of both the company and the client.

---

[23] Be an EPIC Defender of PII-Keep your customers' information safe as you would your own. This eliminates any security risks to the customer as well. It also protects you from being accused of doing something illegal. PII is also known as personally identifiable information.

Most every company will allow you to state in a public form or social network site that you work for them. However, most of the clients do not want you indicating that it is their contract you are working on. This is where the non-disclosure agreement you signed at hire plays an important role. Non-disclosure prevents client procedures from being revealed as well as the fact that they outsource to agents that work from home. While it may seem taboo that companies do not want to reveal that they use at home agents, it is more for protection. Most customers are not friendly to the fact that a customer service or tech support representative is looking at their private information while in the comfort of their own home. Not everyone has the correct interpretation of what it is like to be a WAH Professional and you have to protect that. Many larger companies want to project the most professional light about their work force and procedures. Traditional customers tend to view WAH agents as less than professional and not as secure as someone in an office building where they can be strongly supervised. Therefore, revealing to a client that you work from home is not in the best interest of any party involved. Pay close attention to your non-disclosure agreement. You sign this in your new hire packet and it is very important. It may even have clauses that dictate what your rights are upon termination of your employment as well as time constraints concerning working for a competing company. Any questions should be directed to your HR representative. Make sure you are willing and able to abide by the terms in the non-disclosure agreement. Failure to do so could result in fines and penalties should the company or client pursue legal action. This is not meant to scare you. It is only intended to protect you and the company from competitors and clients wanting to gain advantage over your employer. If you are certain you are unable to abide by the terms, then a different position or WAH company should be considered.

When things go wrong

There will come a day, as a WAH Professional, that everything will go wrong. Whether it is power, phone or Internet issues, or your work tools do not function properly, it will happen. These times will try all of your patience and make you feel like the best thing to do is quit and find something else. This is certainly not the answer. When things get rough, do not just pack up and leave! Remember, it happens to everyone and at every work place. Keep in mind the following tips when these times happen and, before you know it, your workday will return to normal:

1. This is not how it normally is. It is just a bump in the road. You know that the normal routine is much easier.
2. If you are able to clock in, you are getting paid. On top of that, most companies will still pay you if A, you are scheduled to work and B, if it is their systems that are causing the issue.
3. It WILL get better. While it may take 24-48 hours for the issue to be resolved, most companies have great IT departments and getting their systems back online is what they do. Patience is a virtue.
4. Remember that it is not like being in the same room with a horrible boss or rude co-workers. Your systems have taken a temporary slide and will soon return back to normal.

The important thing to remember is to wait out this inconvenience. It may work out in your favor. If you can get through a trying time like this and still have your job, it looks good for you when you decide to try for that promotion or move to a different program. It is even helpful to mention it when applying for different job types within the same company. Further, if your supervisor can be put down as a reference for future job endeavors, it will be something good they can note about you to a potential employer. Things happen and times get rough from time to time. Just remember, it will get better.

Family and children

Having family and friends whom never worked at home before can provide a challenge to any WAH Professional. They should respect your position and understand the boundaries that have been set. Compliance to these set boundaries can mean the difference in whether you keep your job or not. As stated before, many people have an incorrect interpretation of what it means to be a WAH agent. Whether it is the fact that you are not allowed to bring someone on a job with you while delivering phone books or the absolute no background noise rule, it must be made clear to friends and family that they do not disturb you while working. Having a conversation with the people that try to interrupt you (while working) is of vital importance and should not be overlooked. Nothing is more upsetting to have a loud dinner party going on in the next room or to have a family member let a friend in so they can "see you" while you are at work. It is unprofessional and can cost you your job.

If you have children, it is even more important for them to know that, even though you are at home, you are still at work and they should pretend you are not there. (Unless, of course, there is an emergency.) Your sitter can help you with keeping the errant child occupied while you are working. To help my children understand the difference between sitting at my desk paying bills and sitting at my desk working, I would randomly put on my headset and sit at my desk. The fact that I have my headset on indicates to them that I should not be disturbed. Even though my door is open, I still may be getting ready to work. This helped them learn when not to disturb me. After about eight months as a WAH Agent, my youngest got the picture. I decided I wanted to be alone with my thoughts and see which of my family members knew the boundaries. I sat down at my desk and started to check my email. Normally I do this and my family can come in, sit with me or talk to me and it is no problem. This time however, I put my headset on and left the door open. The first one to come in was the baby of the family. I am proud to say that, he came around the corner into my office and seen that I had my headset on. Immediately, he about faced, and quietly walked away. Our son knew that because I "looked" like I was working, he had to quietly go to Daddy and not disturb Mommy. That was a proud Mommy moment as well as a WAH Professional moment. I knew my family understood the work boundaries.

Pro Tips

Every job has its specifics and challenges. There are some tips that I can provide to help you become the best you can while working from home. As stated earlier in this book, most jobs evaluate you on specific measurements and goals called metrics. This section provides you some tips to assist in getting the metric scores improved and quite possibly, making you look like a "rock star" of your team.

Calls per hour: How many calls you take in one-hour increments. Many companies will dictate to you how long the average call should be or the maximum time you should spend on a call. This metric allows the company to provide services to more than one customer per hour per agent. One such example would be that you are required to take at least 4-5 calls an hour and each call should be about eight to ten minutes or less. This actually covers two metrics but if you are striving for the 8-10 minute calls then you will definitely reach the goal of 4 to 5 call an hour. Keep in mind that slow business times will prevent you from achieving that when you only answer 2 or 3 calls in an hour. If you are doing your job, the call length will become acceptable. Also, if you do not waste time between calls, then you will always be available for the next call when it comes in. Your supervisors will adjust staffing levels during slow times to ensure you are getting calls in a timely manner. This is why there are volunteer or mandatory jump offs. Further, you do not want to be too far above the calls per hour because it could be viewed that you are not taking enough time with each customer you interact with. If you are not taking enough time with your customers, it can hurt customer satisfaction and (worst case) they may take their business elsewhere.

Customer Satisfaction Surveys: Almost every company wants to know what their customers think of the representatives they interact with during business operations. While this is likely directly tied to an overall opinion of the company, customers will fill out surveys about their interactions with you. While not always positive, you can do your best to ensure the customer does not leave the call with you in an angry manner or with a bad impression. Companies vary on how much emphasis they place on this. Be mindful of how you treat the customers no matter what. You want their interaction with you to be positive. Anything you can do to make their opinion of the company better will go far in making your Customer Survey scores stellar.

Average Talk Time: This is how much time you spend on the phone with the customer. As stated before, companies will dictate to you how long a customer interaction should be. For phone representatives, it averages about 8-10 minutes maximum per call. Sometimes a call will go far beyond that while others will be way less. So long as your average is within acceptable limits, you can be assured you are doing your job within the time constraints provided. This goes hand in hand with Calls per hour. Keeping the customer focused on the reason for their call and minimizing unnecessary chit chat goes a long way in ensuring you are meeting this metric.

Along the same lines, many call centers want you to minimize any "dead air" during a call. Dead air is where the customer is waiting for you to type something or find an answer. This will come with practice and helps keep the call focused on the reason the customer called in.

Call percentage: Nearly all companies will measure this. This is the amount of time of your scheduled workday that you are physically on a call with a customer. This enables the company to predict call volume and schedule agents accordingly. It also enables the company to find the agents that are wasting time or riding the clock. If the goal is to be at 80% or higher and you are only achieving 44%, then something is not right. This means you are spending a lot of idle time doing something you should not be doing or avoiding calls. For nearly all call centers, avoiding calls is a terminable offense. If you find you are falling well below the talk percentage, and you are always available to take calls, you may want to change your schedule around to work on busier days or during a time of day when more calls are coming in.

Idle time: Idle time is time that you spend on breaks, or do not disturb time used to make extra notes on an account after the allotted time to do so have expired. This should be used sparingly and avoided if at all possible. If you are allowed to take breaks then this is just about the only part of idle time that is acceptable. Companies want idle time to only be about 3-5% of your total hours worked. No matter how much you work, this is not a lot of time. When you first start working, you will probably use a lot of idle time wrapping up a call. This expected. The more experience you have in doing your job, the less idle time you will use to wrap up a call. Keeping within this metric is easy to accomplish once you get to know your job well. This is because you will have learned to take notes and check everything during the call and not have to do anything but close the customers' record upon the customer disconnecting.

First Call Resolve: Resolving all of customers' issues during your call is paramount to their perception of the company and how its customer service is rated. This metric measures how many times your caller will call back after talking to you regarding the same issue or other issues. It can also measure how many times the customer calls back in a measured time period. Some companies measure 7-day callbacks as well as 30-day callbacks. While some customers call for every little thing, others will greatly appreciate the fact that you attempt to cover all bases before letting them go. Many companies want their first call resolve number to be 80% or better because first call resolve is closely related to customer experience. The better the customer feels about the experience they have with the company, the more likely they will remain loyal customers. They will also likely refer this company to friends and family. Having to call back for a same or similar issue can be a burden. It makes the experiences worse if the customer has to navigate an automated phone system before speaking to an actual representative. If you attempt to resolve all immediate issues, the customer may not have reason to call back in the next thirty days and will be quite happy with the resolution you provided them.

Call documentation: All customer experiences should be documented. Sometimes, there are calls that are not documented. This should be minimal. Of course there will be calls when there is no one there. Other times, there will be callers who cannot provide you with any information to successfully pull up an account. Your company will provide you a way to document the session every single time your phone rings. This is one of the easiest metrics to keep high. If you are unsure how to document a specific issue, consult your team lead for clarification.

Short calls vs. long calls: Quite a few companies have reports that are generated for calls that are less than 2 minutes. Conversely, there are reports for calls that last a lot longer than they should. If you are having calls that are showing up frequently on the short call report, then it may be interpreted that you are not meeting customer expectations. Be wary that most companies will take at least 2-3 minutes with a customer to simply verify the account before attempting to resolve the issue. Do your best to keep your overly short calls to a minimum. Long calls can be viewed as call avoidance. Long calls can be listened to and it can be determined if you are wasting time or putting the customer on hold too much. Keep within protocols while handling customer issues. If you are having issues where you are taking too many long calls, discuss it with your team lead so they can help you get your call times down.

Percentage schedule worked: You want to work your schedule as it is set out for you. Missing work reduces the numbers here and you do not want to come across as not wanting to work. While no agent will adhere 100% exactly, it can make a difference if your team leader is ranking your team by their metrics. Further, those high performing agents are often those that show up and work their set schedules everyday. Of course things happen and you may have to miss work. You can make that up by improving your attendance after such an emergency.

Graded calls or QA: This ensures you are following procedures for opening and closing the call. You are graded on ensuring you are validating the account properly. You are also evaluated on the tools you use and the documentation of the call. These help you figure out what your strengths and weaknesses are and provide good insight to what policies you need to review. Take to heart the suggestions in the graded calls and put them to use as soon as possible. Some repeat offenses may look bad and they are used to assist you in becoming better at your job.

While not all inclusive, the above metrics are measured and are often used in determining your chances for raises, promotions, and lateral moves within the company. Some things to keep in mind are as follows:

1. Keep up with all policies and procedures used in the capacity of your job. The callers that have issues that are common will become easier to resolve. Any change in policy can hinder the resolution of that issue so keep the information you have up to date.
2. As you get better at your job, it will become easier to keep your notes and information one step ahead of what you are actually doing. This involves multitasking and anticipating what can happen next.
3. Always refer to available knowledge bases and information for items to address for every call. Most companies will have a script or virtual library for you to refer to when resolving a customers' issue.
4. When asking for help, clearly state the customers' issue, what tools you

used and where you looked for the right answer. Coaches and supervisors want to know that you have covered all bases before seeking help as most answers are provided within the tools available. While not every situation will be found, they can better utilize their time by helping resolve complicated issues over simple issues that you should have resolved on your own.

5. By staying one or two steps ahead of what you are actually doing, it eliminates the time you have to wait to find out an answer or get an approval. Team leaders and coaches are doing other things besides waiting for you to ask a question. Sometimes, there may be a delay in their response. For example: You have a customer who has to turn their TV around to look at the back. What they find dictates the next step in the process. If their cables are incorrectly hooked up, you can refer to the diagram and assist accordingly. If they are using the wrong cables or ones you are not familiar with, you can advise them properly or post a question to the coach. If you post the question about a dated cable and what its replacement should be before the customer asks you, then you are one step ahead of them. By the time the coach responds, you will then have a timely answer to provide to the customer without having to waste any of the customers' time.

6. Pay attention to the assistance provided to other agents. You may have the same question in the future and if you note it

as something important, you may be able to quickly resolve a similar issue more quickly than waiting for a response from a coach. This help metrics all around.

7. Reread common articles as they change often. Policies are updated everyday and you want to make sure you are following the right procedure. You don't want to be called on a policy that you thought was right when the last time you read the policy was six months ago. It could have been updated weekly during that period and you would not know it if you do not review it once in a while.

8. As stated before, pay attention to your reviews and your quality checks on your calls. Making a conscious effort in improving the deficiencies will go far in making you the best you can be at your job.

Final note

This world has become smaller and larger at the same time. People are working form home in more ways than ever before. Long gone are the Bell operators that had large phone board on their kitchen tables' connecting neighbor to neighbor. There are customer service centers that assist callers on the other side of the world as well as right next door. While many people still go out the front door to work every day, there are more than you think who remain at home and work from the office in the next room. Just as professional as the ones sitting in a cubicle on the tenth floor, WAH Professionals are leading their lives in a very different way than the rest of the working world. This book was meant to introduce you to the lifestyle of working from home. While not all-inclusive, it attempts to inform you of the things you may encounter when they start to look for and ultimately work as an at home worker. Not all jobs are the same just as each of us are individuals.

WAH is a lifestyle and can be just as fulfilling as any other career choice. Welcome to my world. Welcome to the world where your workers are thousands of miles away as well as right next-door. This is the virtual work world. You can make friends, network, and encounter countless job leads from the comfort of your floppy puppy slippers. Are you ready? Take this book with you to help you decide. Working from home is not for everyone. If you decide that you want to walk out the door everyday and go to work, it is truly a personal choice. Thanks for joining us on this journey anyway. For the rest of you, be ready for your ride. It will make you or grow you. The choice is yours. Welcome to the world of a WAH Professional.

Acknowledgements

This would not have been possible without the constant support of my family. They have put up with my colorfully worded outbursts for noise and spilling my coffee on the keyboard. They have educated friends and visiting family on the nuances of visiting while I am working. They have tested me and supported me in every way. Without my family, I would not have been successful in becoming a WAH Professional.

My husband, Calvin, sat and listened to me rant about the editing process and all the random ideas that popped out of my head while writing this book. My children, Douglas and Alyssa were wonderfully patient as I used their computer A LOT to do my writing and editing. They gave up many hours while I sat and filled up pages and pages only to redo every word. My son Joshua gets his own thank you because, during the evolution of this book, he taught me to love the library again. Without rediscovering the love of a good read, there would be a lot more grammatical errors than you have already found. I also want to thank my Mother who listened in disbelief as I told her over and over again that I was writing a book.

Outside my family, there are others who I attribute inspiration and gratitude. As always, my favorite author, Stephen King receives his own accolades. His stories kept me entertained from an early age. Setting the standard high, he is a great inspiration. A new favorite author, Cinda Williams Chima, allowed me to step outside of the box and see things from a new light. For a long time it was hard for me to read outside of the horror genre and her stories inspired me to take a step into the unknown. That unknown helped bring life to the stories bouncing around in my head just dying to get out. I am also grateful to my grammar Nazi. We all have one. They push us to question the sentence on the screen and possibly rewrite it for the rest of the world to understand our thinking process.

Finally, nothing in this book is possible without my co-workers and the companies that enabled me to work at home. My fellow WAH Professionals that keep the dream alive and, most of all, enabled me to keep my sanity while tethered to my computer for hours on end. For those that contributed suggestions who wanted to be named and those, who did not. This book was possible without you. Finally, to all the companies that took a chance on me and taught me so many things that make up an integral part of the fabric that makes us all WAH professionals. You took a step where most would not venture and opened up a new modern workplace. This has enabled some of us to provide for our families when there were no other options. Thank YOU.

www.ingramcontent.com/pod-product-compliance
Lightning Source LLC
Chambersburg PA
CBHW051732170526
45167CB00002B/899